Thinking Critically

Thinking Critically:
Racial Justice

Olivia Karson

ReferencePoint
Press®

San Diego, CA

© 2023 ReferencePoint Press, Inc.
Printed in the United States

For more information, contact:
ReferencePoint Press, Inc.
PO Box 27779
San Diego, CA 92198
www.ReferencePointPress.com

LIBRARY OF CONGRESS CATALOGING-IN-PUBLICATION DATA

Names: Karson, Olivia, author.
Title: Thinking critically: racial justice / Olivia Karson.
Description: San Diego : ReferencePoint Press, 2023. | Series: Thinking critically
| Includes bibliographical references and index.
Identifiers: LCCN 2021009649 (print)| ISBN
   9781678204624 (library binding) | ISBN 9781678204631 (ebook)
Subjects: LCSH: Racial justice--United States--Juvenile literature.
   Literature. Anti-racism--United States--Juvenile literature. | Social
   justice--United States--Juvenile literature.

Contents

"Literacy is the most basic currency of the knowledge economy we're living in today." Barack Obama (at the time a senator from Illinois) spoke these words during a 2005 speech before the American Library Association. One question raised by this statement is: What does it mean to be a literate person in the twenty-first century?

E.D. Hirsch Jr., author of *Cultural Literacy: What Every American Needs to Know*, answers the question this way: "To be culturally literate is to possess the basic information needed to thrive in the modern world. The breadth of the information is great, extending over the major domains of human activity from sports to science."

But literacy in the twenty-first century goes beyond the accumulation of knowledge gained through study and experience and expanded over time. Now more than ever literacy requires the ability to sift through and evaluate vast amounts of information and, as the authors of the Common Core State Standards state, to "demonstrate the cogent reasoning and use of evidence that is essential to both private deliberation and responsible citizenship in a democratic republic."

The Thinking Critically series challenges students to become discerning readers, to think independently, and to engage and develop their skills as critical thinkers. Through a narrative-driven, pro/con format, the series introduces students to the complex issues that dominate public discourse—topics such as gun control and violence, social networking, and medical marijuana. All chapters revolve around a single, pointed question such as Can Stronger Gun Control Measures Prevent Mass Shootings?, or Does Social Networking Benefit Society?, or Should Medical Marijuana Be Legalized? This inquiry-based approach introduces student researchers to core issues and concerns on a given topic. Each chapter includes one part that argues the affirmative and one part that argues the negative—all written by a single author. With the single-author format the predominant arguments for and against an issue can be synthesized into clear, accessible discussions supported by details and evidence including relevant facts, direct quotes, current examples, and statistical illustrations. All volumes include focus questions to guide students as they read each pro/con discussion, a list of key facts, and an annotated list of related organizations and websites for conducting further research.

The authors of the Common Core State Standards have set out the particular qualities that a literate person in the twenty-first century must have. These include the ability to think independently, establish a base of knowledge across a wide range of subjects, engage in open-minded but discerning reading and listening, know how to use and evaluate evidence, and appreciate and understand diverse perspectives. The new Thinking Critically series supports these goals by providing a solid introduction to the study of pro/con issues.

Racial Justice

In May 2020 a smartphone recorded a video that would set the world ablaze. Captured on camera was White Minneapolis police officer Derek Chauvin kneeling on the neck of a Black man named George Floyd for over nine minutes—including three minutes after Floyd lost consciousness. It was, many people argued, one of the most flagrant displays of racialized police violence in recent years. Following the viral video, tweets expressing support for Black lives came in the hundreds of millions. Opinion polls conducted around this time showed that up to 70 percent of Americans believed that Black people and other minorities were being denied equal treatment in society. In that year alone, an estimated 20 million people in the United States took part in protests against racial discrimination—particularly as presented in the criminal justice system.

Conversations about racial justice took place both before and after Floyd's death. In 2016, for example, the Standing Rock Sioux Tribe sued in federal court to stop construction of a major oil pipeline project that threatened the tribe's water supply. That action garnered unprecedented support from more than two hundred tribes. In another instance, over sixty rallies took place on a single day in 2021 to protest the nearly four thousand hate crimes committed against Asian Americans amid tensions brought about by the COVID-19 pandemic. Countless more issues of discrimination have thrust the conversation of racial justice into the spotlight.

What Is Racial Justice?

Racial justice refers to fair treatment and equal opportunities for all people, regardless of race. To achieve racial justice, society must commit to ongoing structural and systemic support for equal access to opportunities and elimination of race-based disparities. In a racially just world, bias would not impact anyone's ability to be safe or successful.

But bias still exists—and racism remains a reality in the United States. Sometimes racism is overt, or easy to see. Particularly striking was a 2017 rally of White nationalists in Charlottesville, Virginia. As they marched, they shouted chants of "Jews will not replace us" and "Blood and soil," a trope stemming from Nazi Germany. It refers to the idea that only those of Aryan descent could own and farm land. In 2022, moreover, one county in Mississippi reported the circulation of Ku Klux Klan fliers in its neighborhoods. The Klan, a White racist organization founded after the Civil War, has long engaged in intimidation, violence, and murder.

Microaggressions

Instances like these involve clear and intentional racism, but racist ideas can also manifest in less obvious ways. Most common today are microaggressions. Microaggressions are subtle, everyday actions that communicate some form of bias against a particular group, often unintentionally. Derald Wing Sue is an Asian American professor of psychology from Oregon. He describes this kind of everyday racism as it occurs in his own life: "I get verbal microaggressions all the time. After I do an address, audience members will compliment me and say, 'You speak excellent English.' And while the person means it to be a compliment, the underlying communication is that I am a perpetual alien in my own country. I am not a true American."[1]

Verbiage like this still reinforces racial divides, even as seven out of ten Americans report that they are angry that racism still

In San Francisco in 2021 protesters march against violence and discrimination aimed at Asian Americans. Since the COVID-19 pandemic, incidents of discrimination and violence targeting Asian Americans have risen.

exists, according to a national study by the University of Massachusetts in 2022. Microaggressions are—by definition—small, but they have the power to escalate into more dangerous forms of racism. This happened during the COVID-19 pandemic. Research suggests that the pandemic originated in China. Some segments of the public saw this as an excuse to launch verbal attacks on Americans of Asian descent. Certain politicians and members of the media encouraged xenophobic attitudes by repeatedly referring to COVID-19 as a "Chinese virus" or "kung flu." There were also many reported incidents of strangers walking up to Asian Americans and yelling insults about bringing sickness to America and, in some cases, even issuing death threats.

These racially charged interactions were not happening on a small scale. By 2021 82 percent of Ipsos poll respondents said that they had witnessed discrimination against Asian Americans as a result of pandemic scapegoating. By the end of that year, National

Public Radio (NPR) had documented over nine thousand incidents against Asian Americans, from microaggressions to outright physical assaults and murder. Warren Ng, a psychiatrist, explains:

> How does something as little as name calling lead to something like murder? That seems like a big jump. But there's a pathway to that action and understanding where microaggressions, racism, dehumanization, objectification, stereotyping, and all of those things lead to us distancing ourselves and our humanity from that other person who is a human being. The more that they are not a human being, the more that we're able to feel that we can do things to them because they're not the same as you and I.[2]

Equality Versus Equity

Americans recognize the problems that this country still faces regarding race. In 2021 one Ipsos poll asked almost two thousand American adults whether they agreed with the statement "America is not a racist country." Fewer than one in four agreed.

However, not everyone agrees on what racial justice should look like. Part of this disagreement involves the debate of equality versus equity. Equality refers to equal treatment, meaning people of all races should be treated the same in society, with no group given preferential treatment over another. Equity, on the other hand, refers not to the fairness of how people are treated but to fairness in the outcomes each group experiences. People who follow the equity approach believe that preferential treatment can be okay to give to certain people if their race has given them a disadvantage. In both approaches, the goal is for all to be treated fairly.

"Microaggressions, racism, dehumanization, objectification, stereotyping, and all of those things lead to us distancing ourselves and our humanity from that other person who is a human being."[2]

—Warren Ng, psychiatrist

But the ways in which people seek racial justice can differ greatly. One example is when college admissions boards give greater consideration to a Black applicant over a White applicant who has a very similar application. In the equity approach, the admissions board might accept the Black student because Black people were historically denied admissions to colleges until relatively recently, which makes it harder to accrue Black representation in higher education today. In the equality approach, the admissions board would admit the preferable candidate regardless of race, because differential treatment regarding race in any form is wrong and unjust. Both schools of thought are widely represented in the conversation around racial justice today.

Why Is Racial Justice Important?

The United States has always been known as the world's melting pot: a common home for immigrants from all corners of the world. But today the country is diversifying even more rapidly than experts had predicted. In 2019 over half of Americans younger than sixteen identified as a race other than White (scholars sometimes use the umbrella term *BIPOC*—which stands for "Black, Indigenous, and people of color"—to refer to races other than White). Racial lines that were once rigid in society have softened, and such unprecedented levels of diversity make conversations about racial justice not only compelling but constitutionally meaningful.

The equal protection clause of the Fourteenth Amendment requires that state laws apply to all people equally, regardless of race (among other characteristics). While the amendment was initially created to grant formerly enslaved people the same citizenship as White Americans, the concept of equal protection is crucial in addressing more modern forms of racial injustice today. For example, one recently enacted California law required publicly held corporations to include at least one member from an underrepresented community on the board of directors. But the law was short-lived. It was struck down in 2022 by a California Superior Court judge because it involved a quota based on race, which would violate equal treatment of those vying for a position on the board.

The Road Ahead

Conversations about racial justice are taking place around the nation. According to a 2021 Pew Research Center poll, nine in ten Americans say that the country has made progress toward equality of race over the past fifty years. Others, as documented in a 2020 Ipsos poll, say that racial justice has stalled, with only one in three respondents believing that recent efforts toward equality have led to meaningful results. Staggering discrepancies between the experiences of White Americans and other Americans still exist in the economy, the criminal justice system, and other facets of daily life. People of all walks of life are eager to see how the country addresses these inequalities. As Theodore R. Johnson of the Brennan Center for Justice, a nonprofit public policy institute, says, "We cannot realize justice in America unless we are willing to confront racism. There is no way around it. There is no shortcut."[3]

> "We cannot realize justice in America unless we are willing to confront racism. There is no way around it. There is no shortcut."[3]
>
> —Theodore R. Johnson, fellow at the Brennan Center for Justice

Chapter One

Is Racial Bias Preventing Some Americans from Achieving Economic Progress?

Racial Bias Prevents Some Americans from Achieving Economic Progress

- Housing discrimination makes it more likely for people of color to be trapped in impoverished areas, making it difficult to access quality community resources and create intergenerational wealth.
- Discriminatory lending by American banks prevents people of color from affording housing, tuition, business start-ups, and other high-cost investments at the same rate as White loan applicants.
- White people receive higher wages, on average, than their non-White counterparts. This undervalued labor costs Americans billions in forgone wages.

The Debate at a Glance

Racial Bias Is Not the Cause of Lack of Economic Progress

- While discrimination may exist in the workplace, employment patterns are the true determinants of wealth and wages.
- Government aid and private donations alike have afforded trillions of dollars to people of color in need, an indicator of good faith and togetherness on the road to economic justice for all.
- Economic outcomes vary between and within races, suggesting that racial bias alone cannot explain discrepancies in wealth.

Racial Bias Prevents Some Americans from Achieving Economic Progress

"The entire premise of the American Dream is based on the myth of a meritocracy. If it were in fact a meritocracy, race-based chasms in wages, unemployment rates, home ownership rates and so many other indicators of economic well-being would not exist."

—April Taylor, Kentucky-based activist

April Taylor, "No Matter How Smart or Hard-Working, Racism Makes the American Dream a Myth for Many," *Lexington (KY) Herald-Leader*, February 19, 2021. www.kentucky.com.

Consider these questions as you read:

1. What is the connection between where a person lives and economic progress? Explain your answer.
2. In what ways do loans help people accumulate wealth?
3. Some groups earn more money than other groups. Is this a sign of a free market, or is it evidence that some groups face some disadvantage? Explain your answer.

Editor's note: The discussion that follows presents common arguments made in support of this perspective, reinforced by facts, quotes, and examples taken from various sources.

In 1951 African American poet Langston Hughes asked, "What happens to a dream deferred? Does it dry up like a raisin in the sun?"[4] He was referencing the American dream, the idea that anyone—from any background—can become successful if they take advantage of the ample opportunities in American life. But Hughes was questioning the legitimacy of this dream and whether its promises truly do apply to people of all races.

These same questions still apply today, with certain groups accumulating more and more wealth while other groups are unable to do so. According to the Federal Reserve, in 2020 the average White family had over four times the wealth of the average

Hispanic family and eight times the wealth of the average Black family. While explicit economic discrimination—such as paying a lower wage based on race alone—has been illegal for a long time, these gaps in economic progress reflect the racial injustice still permeating life in America.

Housing

Housing is one of the biggest predeterminants of wealth, for several reasons. For most people, their home is the most valuable asset they own. As the home increases (or appreciates) in value over time, the homeowner's wealth increases too. Second, housing determines access to community-funded resources, including schooling, health care, law enforcement and first responders, and more. However, not all Americans have equal access to home ownership—and the accrual of wealth that comes with it.

Redlining is one public policy that continues to affect today's patterns of racialized homeownership. In the 1900s, governments expanded the use of lending programs to boost homeownership and its benefits. Officials color coded maps of over two hundred US cities to decide which areas qualified for government funding. The highest-qualifying areas were colored green and consisted mostly of safe, clean suburbs full of White families. The red-colored areas that did not qualify, on the other hand, were poor areas concentrated with people of color—hence the term *redlining*. As Richard Rothstein from the Economic Policy Institute notes, today's enormous difference in wealth between races "is almost entirely attributable to federal housing policy implemented through the 20th century."[5] Not unlike the forceful displacement of Native Americans into federally set reservations, redlining and other racially discriminatory housing policies have America's racial minorities concentrated in low-income housing areas with underfunded schools and greater crime.

Even today racial discrimination continues to exert a strong influence on where people can live. In 2021 researchers for the National Bureau of Economic Research published the largest study to date on discrimination in the housing market. In the study, economists sent inquiries from fictional renters to over eight thousand property managers in the United States, using fake names that were considered stereotypically White, Black, or Hispanic. The researchers found that the White-sounding names received almost 5 percent more responses than the Hispanic-sounding names and 9 percent more responses than the Black-sounding names.

These instances add up. In 2018 alone, over eight thousand fair housing complaints were filed on allegations of racial discrimination. Countless others go unreported. One Black woman in Virginia recalls asking a landlord about a rental property listed online. The landlord, meaning to message the current renters, sent back to her, "She's definitely African. I don't want her in the group house."[6] Sharing her story, the woman explains, "His racist assumptions about my desirability as a tenant resulted in me experiencing homelessness, to leave school before I could complete my associate's degree and it has deeply hurt me emotionally."[7]

> "[The landlord's] racist assumptions about my desirability as a tenant resulted in me experiencing homelessness, to leave school before I could complete my associate's degree and it has deeply hurt me emotionally."[7]
>
> —Anonymous Black woman in Virginia

Banking

Racial bias can also be found in the banking industry. Discriminatory loan practices by banks mean that people of color are less likely to qualify for loans, which are almost always required for home ownership, paying tuition, or starting a business. All of these are considered investments toward financial security. If Whites are more likely to qualify for these loans, then they benefit from the advantages of loans in ways that non-Whites do not.

Take mortgages, for example, which are loans for home or land ownership. The Associated Press conducted a national study of over 2 million mortgage applications in 2021. Data reporters Emmanuel Martinez and Lauren Kirchner explain:

> We found that lenders were 40 percent more likely to turn down Latino applicants for loans, 50 percent more likely to deny Asian/Pacific Islander applicants, and 70 percent more likely to deny Native American applicants than similar White applicants. Lenders were 80 percent more likely to reject Black applicants than similar White applicants. . . . In every case, the prospective borrowers of color looked almost exactly the same on paper as the White applicants, except for their race.[8]

It is not clear whether these staggering discrepencies are due to overt discrimination or more subtle biases held by banks and lenders. But the economic losses caused by discriminatory lending are clear. A 2020 study by Citigroup calculated the financial blows that occur when African Americans fail to qualify for loans. The researchers estimate that discriminatory lending has prevented African Americans from generating $218 billion in wealth from homeownership, $113 billion in lifetime income from a college degree, and $13 trillion in business revenue from start-ups—which would also have created over 6 million jobs. These discrepancies are real, extraordinary in magnitude, and decidedly racial.

Wage Gap

A conversation about bias in the economy would not be complete without discussing the wage gap. A wage gap is a difference in average earnings of one group compared to another group. Traditional conversations about the wage gap have referred to differences in gender, because the overall average earnings of men in the United States far exceed the average earnings of women. These differences are also present when the earnings of White people are compared to those of other races.

Discrimination Leads to Wide Gaps in Household Wealth

The total wealth of White households far outpaces that of Black and Hispanic households in the United States. Wealth accumulates over time as people make and benefit from investments like homeownership. Because of discriminatory practices, these types of investments are often not available to Black and Hispanic Americans. In this way, the economic gap between White households and non-White households widens over time.

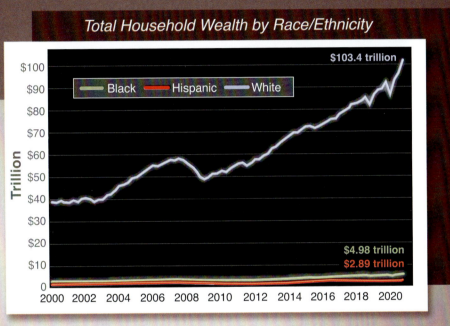

Total Household Wealth by Race/Ethnicity

Legend: Black — Hispanic — White

$103.4 trillion

$4.98 trillion
$2.89 trillion

Source: Lydia Saad, "Americans' Confidence in Racial Fairness Waning," Gallup, July 30, 2021. https://news.gallup.com.

For example, in 2020 the Economic Policy Institute reported that Black men make seventy-one cents for every dollar paid to White men. Economists often argue that this difference is because work done by people of color is undervalued. It is more difficult for people of color to get hired and promoted into high-earning positions, regardless of their qualifications. In fact, in 2021 financial writer Dion Rabouin found that a White American with only a high school education is just as likely to become a millionaire as a Black American with a master's degree. This suggests that racial bias, not a qualification gap, is preventing minority workers from reaching pay parity with White earners.

And the earnings gap widens further when accounting for gender. Data from the National Partnership for Women & Families found that Black women earned fifty-eight cents for every dollar paid to White men in 2022. Worse still, this number dropped to fifty cents on the dollar for Native American women, and just forty-one cents for Latina women. The Center for American Progress explains, "The stubborn resilience of the gender wage gap, coupled with intersecting racial bias in the workplace, means that many women of color are perpetually underpaid, and these losses accumulate and grow over time. As a result, women of color are less able to build savings, withstand economic downturns, and achieve some measure of economic stability."[9]

This is not news for many women of color, including a Texas-based therapist named Teresa Chavez. Long aware that she was being paid less than her White colleagues, she discussed a pay raise with her supervisor—but she was denied and even given a suggestion for a different, lower-paying job. Chavez says, "You do everything right, everything you're supposed to do to reach the American dream, and it's still not enough."[10]

Racial Bias Is Not the Cause of Lack of Economic Progress

"The truth of the matter is that there is no excuse for the equity doctrine. . . . [Its proponents] don't care at all that there are multiple well-documented reasons for unequal outcomes in occupational choice and pay."

—Jordan B. Peterson, professor and clinical psychologist

Jordan B. Peterson, "Equity: When the Left Goes Too Far," Jordan Peterson (website), May 15, 2019. www.jordanbpeterson.com.

Consider these questions as you read:

1. Should equal representation of races be expected in every job industry? Why or why not?
2. Are government assistance programs enough to address the incidence of poverty among people of color?
3. How accurate is race as a predictor for financial security? What else contributes to better or worse financial outcomes?

Editor's note: The discussion that follows presents common arguments made in support of this perspective, reinforced by facts, quotes, and examples taken from various sources.

Despite today's skepticism surrounding the American dream, countless Americans still have faith in its promises. In 2018 the American Enterprise Institute surveyed a sample of almost twenty-five hundred Americans about their attitudes toward community and society. Participants of all races responded similarly: over 80 percent of White, Black, Hispanic, and Asian respondents said that they had achieved, or were on the path to achieving, the success promised by the American dream. There may still be obstacles to economic progress for some Americans, but the results of this survey strongly suggest that racial bias is not one of them.

Wealth Gaps over Time

Even so, research shows that the wealth of White households has far surpassed that of Black, Hispanic, and Native American households. With historic injustices like slavery so staunchly curbing the accumulation of intergenerational wealth, economic parity across all races requires time. But there is a growing body of evidence that today's economy is serving as that turnaround point. Minority gains in the highest-paying sectors suggest that racial bias may no longer have a significant effect on economic progress.

Part of the reason for the racial wealth gap is that extremely high earners tend to be White. This raises the overall average of White wealth. A 2019 Federal Reserve report explained this using the median (or middle) White wage earner. The report found that 97 percent of White wealth was earned by Americans above this median, and only 3 percent of White wealth was earned below. This makes it difficult to compare the middle White earner to the middle Black earner, for example, when it is predominantly the top White earners who outpace the top Black earners.

Because of this lopsided distribution, 2021 research from McKinsey & Company found that the majority of the racial wealth gap could be explained by just 4 percent of the highest-earning occupations. Doctors and lawyers, for example, earn such high wages that having a concentration of White people in these positions therefore concentrates White wealth. Increasing minority representation in this top 4 percent, researchers say, should dramatically attack the racial wage gap.

This is already happening. Reuters reported in 2021 that in the past decade, the share of lawyers of color went from 11.2 to 14.6 percent—still a modest proportion, but a 30 percent jump nonetheless. Latinos specifically showed a dramatic increase, doubling their representation as lawyers in that period.

The health care sector shows gains for racial minorities as well. In 2021 the United States had its largest spike in the

Americans of All Races Have Faith in the American Dream

The American Dream emphasizes economic mobility: the chance to become successful regardless of one's background. A survey by the conservative public policy research organization AEI found that a majority of people of all races believe they have achieved or will achieve this goal. Positive attitudes consistent across groups suggests that the American economy indeed affords opportunity for all, regardless of race.

Question: The Term "American Dream" can mean different things to different people. However you define it, do you believe . . .?

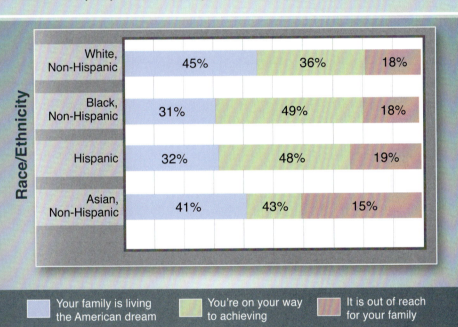

Race/Ethnicity

Group	Your family is living the American dream	You're on your way to achieving	It is out of reach for your family
White, Non-Hispanic	45%	36%	18%
Black, Non-Hispanic	31%	49%	18%
Hispanic	32%	48%	19%
Asian, Non-Hispanic	41%	43%	15%

Source: Samuel J. Abrams et al. "AEI Survey on Community and Society," AEI, February 2019. www.aei.org.

number of Black students enrolled in medical school. Nationally, Black medical students have increased by 21 percent, with one Massachusetts school even tripling the number of first-year Black med students. Other states hope to achieve similar results. New York, for example, has invested over $100 million in historically Black medical schools in order to keep this trend going.

There is still work to be done. But the increase in racial minorities in these high-earning sectors—the 4 percent that causes the majority of the racial wealth gap—is inspiring. Racial bias may have had a grip on the nation's past, but minorities in today's economy attacking racial divides in top-earning jobs is a sign of hope and healing that should not be discounted.

Aid Programs

Others point to the reach of government aid programs as evidence that the US economy promotes racial justice. In the 1960s President Lyndon B. Johnson launched the War on Poverty. This campaign transferred money from the government to low-income households to curb the challenges that come with poverty and in turn help promote economic mobility. Given America's rocky racial history, it is no surprise that many of these transfers were made to BIPOC families.

Since the War on Poverty, about $20 trillion has been spent on these efforts. A 2019 Urban Institute analysis found that, of similar social safety net programs that exist today, African Americans were the racial group most likely to get assistance. About 85 percent of those living in poverty received at least one form of government aid. One such recipient is Tanasia Butler in Mississippi, who lived in public housing and used food stamps while she was working toward her bachelor's degree. Within just a month of graduating, she was financially secure enough to discontinue her benefits. Butler explains, "My goal was always to get off [the programs]. The stigma is that black people are lazy, but those benefits helped me survive. Struggle doesn't have a color."[11]

> "The stigma is that black people are lazy, but those benefits helped me survive. Struggle doesn't have a color."[11]
>
> —Tanasia Butler, Black welfare recipient in Mississippi

Efforts to reduce the number of people living in poverty have seen success. In 2019 the US Census Bureau reported that poverty rates for Blacks and Hispanics alike reached an all-time low. Even private organizations have shifted gears to redistribute wealth to racial minorities. In particular, George Floyd's death spurred overwhelming assistance to struggling people of color. The *Washington Post* reported in 2021 that American corporations committed almost $50 billion to the cause of racial justice following Floyd's murder. Some donated to racial justice organizations, while others funded direct grants to households of color, amounting to over $16,000 for every Black household in extreme poverty. While disparities cannot be solved overnight, widespread evidence shows that Americans are serious about racial economic equality.

Earnings Within Races

As many observers have noted, race is not always an accurate indicator of economic standing. Asian Americans in particular have very high income inequality. This refers to a high concentration of wealth and a high concentration of poverty at the same time. In 2018 the Pew Research Center found that the top 10 percent of Asian American earners made over eleven times the amount of those in the bottom 10 percent. On average, Asian men typically earn $1.15 for every dollar earned by a White male worker, according to a 2019 sample of 1.8 million employees. Overall, Asian Americans collectively earn more than White Americans, even though problems with poverty still persist in that demographic. Here race does not seem to be the factor determining economic success.

It is tempting to view race (and racial bias) as a consistent indicator for outcomes associated with wealth, but Asian Americans show that that is not always the case. For example, Asian Americans hold bachelor's degrees at a rate higher than the average American. College degrees are associated with a higher income and therefore greater wealth. But Asian Americans are also less likely to be homeowners than the average American, which limits the opportunity to accumulate wealth through home appreciation. Race, and the outcomes that follow it, is not a perfect predictor of financial standing.

Similarly, immigration allows us to separate race from economic outcomes. Peter H. Schuck for *National Affairs* uses Black immigrants as an example:

> Black immigrants' economic mobility is much greater than that of blacks born in the United States. The median household income of the rapidly growing cohort of black immigrants is about 30% higher than that of American-born blacks. If systemic racism were the primary driver of blacks' disadvantages in America, we would expect it to hold back this population as well. Yet it seems not to have done so. Causal factors other than systemic racism, then, must be contributing significantly to black disadvantage in areas where it persists.[12]

"Causal factors other than systemic racism, then, must be contributing significantly to black disadvantage in areas where it persists."[12]

—Peter H. Schuck, professor of law at Yale

While social scientists are still working to pinpoint these factors, comparing economic outcomes within races rather than between different races helps determine the extent that bias determines economic outcomes. What is sure is that factors impacting economic justice are likely myriad and multifaceted.

Chapter Two

Does Affirmative Action Promote Racial Justice?

Affirmative Action Promotes Racial Justice

- Affirmative action counteracts racial barriers so that everyone can be on the same playing field.
- Policies that increase the diversity of institutions are shown to have a breadth of positive effects for society at large.
- Affirmative action today will put disadvantaged minorities on the path to equal opportunity in the future, eventually eliminating the need for preferential treatment.

The Debate at a Glance

Affirmative Action Does Not Promote Racial Justice

- Affirmative action sets minorities up for failure by placing them without support into environments with peers who are more prepared than they are.
- All positions should be awarded on the basis of merit alone; even well-intentioned discrimination is still discrimination.
- Affirmative action policies rely on assumptions about applicants based on their race that may not be true in reality.

Affirmative Action Promotes Racial Justice

"Race-conscious admissions mainly reflect a simple truth: The effect of race on opportunity and adversity is profound. And our government and universities would be remiss to overlook that."

—*Daily Californian* editorial board

Editorial board, "CA Should Pass ACA 5, End Prop. 209," *Daily Californian*, June 24, 2022. www.dailycal.org.

Consider these questions as you read:

1. Do you think it is ever fair to give some students preferential treatment over others? Why or why not?
2. In what ways can affirmative action influence working and learning environments?
3. What might be some long-term effects of affirmative action policies?

Editor's note: The discussion that follows presents common arguments made in support of this perspective, reinforced by facts, quotes, and examples taken from various sources.

In the 1960s integrating the US workforce was a colossal challenge. Racial tensions ran so high that President John F. Kennedy signed an executive order requiring employers to hire without bias, hoping that it would boost representation from marginalized groups. The policy was called affirmative action.

Affirmative action policies still guide some educational institutions, workplaces, and government contracting. Applications for college admissions or employment opportunities often include race and ethnicity so that the admissions team can intentionally include underrepresented groups. This way affirmative action policies help diversify schools and workplaces by giving greater consideration to applicants who may otherwise face disadvantage.

President Lyndon B. Johnson was among those who believed that historically disadantaged races deserve the benefits of affirmative action. As he said in a 1965 commencement address at Howard University, "You do not take a person who, for years, has been hobbled by chains and liberate him, bring him up to the starting line of a race and then say, 'You are free to compete with all the others,' and still justly believe that you have been completely fair."[13]

Compensating for Disadvantages

The whole concept of affirmative action is based on the idea that institutions would not naturally be reflective of America's diversity if left to their own devices. On average, White people come from more privileged backgrounds that allow them to accrue qualifications for and interest in certain positions. Perhaps even more difficult to address, hiring officers and admissions boards tend to make their choices in a racially discriminatory way—whether they are aware of it or not.

For starters, huge bodies of evidence show that people of color face barriers to obtaining the qualifications they need in order to be competitive. College admissions serve as one of the most glaring examples. The Center for American Progress explains in a 2019 report:

> Wealth makes it easier for families to relocate to better school districts, purchase test preparation books and classes, and pay or help pay college tuition. But centuries of systemic racism and intergenerational transfers have provided white households with far more wealth than households of color. . . . As a result, students of color (especially black students) are more likely than similarly situated white students to attend underfunded and high-poverty K–12 schools . . . [and] are more likely to fare worse on the indicators of success that colleges evaluate for admission, making it harder for people of color to access top-tier public and private colleges.[14]

Numbers back this up. One educational nonprofit, called Ed-Build, reported in 2019 that majority-White schools collectively received a whopping $23 billion more in government funding than non-majority-White schools.

Furthermore, affirmative action inhibits the ability of hiring offices and admissions boards to act in a biased way. Though the equal protection clause forbids explicit discrimination, anti-Black and anti-Hispanic attitudes can still permeate decision-making processes. In 2019 the *Harvard Business Review* highlighted a study that found that job applications with the name Jamal required eight additional years of experience to be considered as competitively as applications with the name Greg. Other studies even show that White applicants with a criminal history received better treatment than Black applicants without criminal records. Clearly, many hiring processes place Black job applicants at a disadvantage. Until that changes, affirmative action is an essential equalizer.

Positive Outcomes

Affirmative action has also been a boon for high-achieving students who might otherwise have been overlooked. The 2019 Center for American Progress report explains that students of color are 23 percent more likely to be admitted to schools that have affirmative action policies in place. For these students, this preferential treatment can be life changing. University of California, Los Angeles law professor Laura E. Gomez graduated from Harvard University in the 1980s. Gomez went to a non-White-majority high school in Albuquerque, New Mexico. While it was a good school, it did not fit the usual profile of high schools attended by most Harvard applicants. She explains, "I knew affirmative action played a role in my admission, and I thought that was fair because I thought that was bringing me up to the starting line. . . . I felt proud that I had gotten there."[15]

> "I knew affirmative action played a role in my admission, and I thought that was fair because I thought that was bringing me up to the starting line."[15]
>
> —Laura E. Gomez, University of California, Los Angeles law professor

Americans Believe Affirmative Action Is Needed

Most Americans do not think that racial minorities have equal opportunities in employment and housing and thus favor affirmative action programs to help rectify those disparities. A 2021 Gallup poll found that support for affirmative action had reached its highest level since 2001, with 62 percent of respondents saying they favor affirmative action programs for racial minorities.

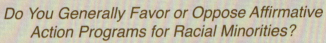

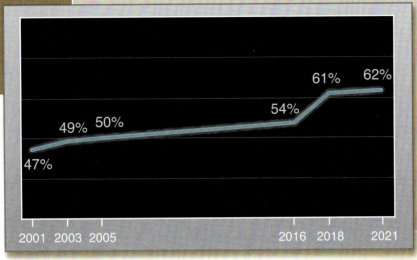

Do You Generally Favor or Oppose Affirmative Action Programs for Racial Minorities?

47% 49% 50% 54% 61% 62%

2001 2003 2005 2016 2018 2021

Source: Lydia Saad, "Americans' Confidence in Racial Fairness Waning," Gallup, July 30, 2021. https://news.gallup.com.

Gomez is just one of many affirmative action success stories. Furthermore, her Harvard admission may have had positive effects on her peers. Research from the Century Foundation, a think tank, suggests that having a racially representative classroom boosts students' intellectual self-confidence, enhances leadership skills, and increases overall classroom satisfaction.

The same is true in the workplace, as was shown in a 2015 study conducted for the *New York Times* by Sheen S. Levine and David Stark. The researchers organized their participants into groups tasked with solving a series of problems. These groups were either racially homogenous or racially diverse. The results were striking: diverse teams were 58 percent more accurate in their answers than the homogenous groups. Levine and Stark reason that these teams performed at such a high level because they disrupted conformity, challenging people to think more critically and originally. The researchers say, "When surrounded by people 'like ourselves,' we are easily influenced, more likely to fall for wrong ideas. Diversity prompts better, critical thinking. It contributes to error detection. It keeps us from drifting toward miscalculation."[16]

In this way, diversity helps everyone—not just minorities. And these better teams translate to more profitable outcomes. Data from Research and Markets in 2021 shows that diverse companies enjoy more than twice the cash flow per employee compared to companies that lack diversity. It is no surprise that 76 percent of 2020 Glassdoor survey respondents said that they consider diversity in choosing an employer. Beyond that, 32 percent stated they would not even apply for a position at a company that lacked a diverse workforce. Americans recognize that a rising tide lifts all boats. For many, affirmative action policies are that rising tide.

Long-Term Solution

Perhaps the most important aspect of affirmative action is that, if implemented correctly, it will not be needed in the long run. Proponents believe that, given enough time to right these racial wrongs, firms and other institutions will no longer need to socially engineer openings for minorities. As put by Ryan Keane for the *Berkeley Political Review*, preferential treatment policies arm "disenfranchised groups with the resources that make them as competitive and economically competent as the white majority so they can never be discriminated against in the future."[17]

Author James E. Cherry describes this idea in the context of the National Basketball Association. He explains:

Each year, the worst 14 teams get the first crack at the best players entering the draft for the upcoming season. This is . . . to bring each individual team up to a competitive level, which in turn elevates the parity and profile of the league. Usually, within a three to four year span, a cellar dweller is vying for the title. Herein lies a message for society as a whole. When all Americans are granted the same opportunities to access the American dream, regardless of race, religion, or ethnicity, then not only does the country live up to its creed, but it becomes a more powerful nation as a whole. This is the promise of America and what makes the country truly great.[18]

Similarly, affirmative action beneficiaries often permanently improve their chances to be competitive in American life—an improvement that transfers to their children, and so on. Breaking the vicious cycle that keeps people of color out of school and out of employment is crucial to the realization of racial justice.

Affirmative Action Does Not Promote Racial Justice

"Affirmative action is antithetical to the American spirit. It is simply unfair that some applicants have to show a greater level of achievement than others to gain admission."

—Arman Sharma, student at Stanford University

Arman Sharma, "Race-Based Affirmative Action Must Be Overturned," *Stanford Review*, March 31, 2022. https://stanfordreview.org.

Consider these questions as you read:

1. Does affirmative action help address racial injustice or perpetuate it? Explain your answer.
2. Is it fair to deny admission to prospective college students who have a higher grade point average and standardized test scores than their admitted peers? Explain your answer.
3. Do you believe that racial bias in the past justifies affirmative action in the present? Explain your answer.

Editor's note: The discussion that follows presents common arguments made in support of this perspective, reinforced by facts, quotes, and examples taken from various sources.

Even among people who believe in the benefits of racial diversity, many remain unconvinced that affirmative action is the right path to take. At its core, race-based affirmative action is about prioritizing one group over another based on ethnicity. Those who obtain admission or jobs through this process frequently endure suspicion of not being quite up to the task, while those who are not chosen are punished for actions that are not their own. Writing for the *New Yorker*, author Louis Menand describes this view from the perspective of some of the detractors of affirmative action. He states their belief that we can ban all forms of preferential treatment and, so long as we enforce existing laws against discrimination, still achieve equality of result. These people see affirmative action as unfairly penalizing those who are not biased themselves and who have enjoyed no personal benefit from discrimination, and they see it as stigmatizing members of underrepresented groups with the suspicion that they are underqualified for the jobs they hold or the school they attend.[19]

In this way systems that differentiate people based on their race—even if well intentioned—may undermine the goal of racial justice.

Setting Minorities Up for Failure

Affirmative action may help minority students at the acceptance stage, but many find that to be far too late. The damage of attending a failing K–12 school remains. Taking students from underfunded public schools and ushering them into an environment of more-prepared peers—and then expecting them to achieve academically the same way—is hardly fair. It is no surprise that minority students who have benefited from affirmative action often fare worse in higher education.

The performance of Black students in law school illustrates this phenomenon. The Heritage Foundation reported in 2015 that in the first year of law school the average African American student (the fiftieth percentile) was performing at the same level as a White student in the fifth percentile. Moreover, almost 20 percent of African American students failed or dropped out, compared to 8 percent of White students. And while 78 percent of White students pass the bar (a test for law students to become licensed lawyers) on their first try, only 57 percent of African Americans pass after any number of attempts. Data from NPR shows that in

2020 White law students still outperformed Black law students on bar exams by an average of eleven points. On a grading scale just sixty points wide, this is actually a vast difference.

This, of course, is not to say that White students are naturally more capable than their non-White peers. But it does illustrate how preferential treatment during the admission decision does not suddenly level the academic playing field. Ryan Keane explains, "Simply increasing minority degree recipients doesn't combat long-term inequality when the educational system doesn't also ensure that disenfranchised students have the underlying academic resources that would make them as competitive once they enter college."[20] In this way affirmative action may provide the appearance of racial justice without promoting it.

Merit

While equal opportunity for people of all races is a laudable goal, elevating one person over another because of race essentially devalues individual achievement, or merit. It is unfair for students who worked hard for a high grade point average, spent time on extracurriculars, and wrote meaningful admissions essays to then be denied entry to a university because they are not the desired race or ethnicity.

OiYan Poon, an Asian American professor of educational policy studies, recalls feeling this on a personal level. Reflecting on her time as a high school student, she says, "I remember hearing at least one teacher say to me, 'It's too bad you're not Black because maybe you would get into a more selective college.'"[21]

Poon is among many who have experienced feelings of invalidation as a result of affirmative action policies. A 2022 Pew Research Center poll of over ten thousand participants found that nearly three in four did not believe that race or ethnicity should be a factor in admissions, including a majority of Black, Hispanic, and Asian respondents. When affirmative action policies were first being implemented in the 1960s, just 4 percent of Black Americans graduated from higher education. In 2019 that was true for over a quarter of Black Americans—a sevenfold increase. While there is still parity to be achieved, many feel that the injustices of a segregated past no longer have a grip on society strong enough to justify race-based policy intervention. Journalist Chris Talgo states:

> Education admissions and hiring should be based on merit, not minority status. The only impartial approach that ensures people are not mistreated because of their race is a merit-based model. . . . In 1961, it would be hard to argue against the need to address institutionalized discrimination. . . . [But] 60 years later, those policies are no longer beneficial to society. In fact, they in many cases create frustration and feelings of unfairness among other groups.[22]

Critics of affirmative action do not necessarily object to increased opportunity for minorities. Instead, some prefer policies that help diversify the applicant pool in the first place, increasing competitiveness across all races. For example, one software company called System Applications & Products in Data Processing started a partnership through Project Propel that offered technology training and skills development to students from historically Black colleges and universities. In this partnership, institutions worked together to create a pipeline to ensure that marginalized communities obtain stable and meaningful employment. By cultivating skills in underserved communities, the applicant pool naturally diversifies, and the need for preferential treatment vanishes. This is a much more direct route to racial justice than race-based affirmative action.

"In 1961, it would be hard to argue against the need to address institutionalized discrimination. . . . [But] 60 years later, those policies are no longer beneficial to society. In fact, they in many cases create frustration and feelings of unfairness among other groups."[22]

—Chris Talgo, journalist

Race-Based Affirmative Action Hurts Asian American Students

The University of North Carolina (UNC) is being sued for discriminatory treatment of Asian American applicants due to affirmative action. According to a 2022 brief by the Asian American Coalition for Education, an in-state Asian American male applicant with a 25 percent statistical likelihood of acceptance to UNC (based on objective measures such as grades) would have a 63 percent chance of acceptance if treated as Hispanic and an 88 percent chance of acceptance if treated as Black. Such disparate treatment based on race alone cannot be considered just.

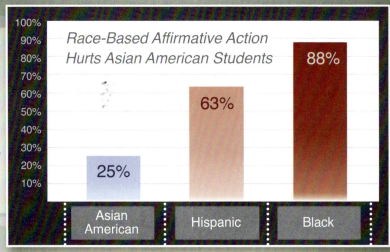

Source: "Over 360 Asian and Other American Organizations Filed Amicus Brief, Jointly Urge the Supreme Court to Ban Anti-Asian Discrimination in College Admissions," Asian American Coalition for Education, May 9, 2022. https://asianamericanforeducation.org.

Race as a Monolith

Others understand the value of preferential policies but disagree that race is the proper metric to use. Racial preferences assume that all members of a group face the same resource advantage or disadvantage, which is not true. Asian Americans serve as a particularly compelling example. As a whole, they are the most educated racial group in the United States. Chinese and Indian Americans graduate from higher education at extraordinary rates. But only 27 percent of Vietnamese Americans hold a bachelor's degree or higher; the same is true for just 17 percent of Hmong

Americans. Under the common label "Asian American," admissions boards fail to consider these backgrounds individually.

Harvard University, for one, is facing extraordinary backlash for its use of racial preferences in admission, a case that was to be heard by the US Supreme Court in 2022. The argument is that racial preference policies discriminate against high-performing Asian Americans in order to accept other minorities, like presumably underserved Black and Hispanic applicants. Plaintiffs cite the fact that the average Asian American Harvard applicant scores 25 points higher than White applicants, 153 points higher than Hispanic applicants, and 217 points higher than Black applicants on the SAT. Despite these lower scores, analysis from Duke University economist Peter Arcidiacono confirms that Harvard accepts about half of prospective Hispanic students and two-thirds of prospective Black students. Harrison Chen is among the Asian American students denied admission to Harvard despite outperforming applicants of other races on standardized tests. He claims that admissions officials "just lumped me into the Asian category, and . . . were not willing to look at us as individuals."[23]

> "Race-based affirmative action fails when it favors minority students who don't have a resource disadvantage over those who do."[24]
>
> —Ryan Keane, writer for the *Berkeley Political Review*

Of course, those in charge of admissions use racial preference policies with the intention of helping underprivileged students. But in 2020, 71 percent of incoming Black and Latino students at Harvard came from wealthy backgrounds. Conversely, 40 percent of Hmong applicants are classified as living below the poverty line. Here, the irony of race-based affirmative action becomes clear. As put by Keane, "Race-based affirmative action fails when it favors minority students who don't have a resource disadvantage over those who do."[24]

Chapter Three

Is the Criminal Justice System Racially Biased?

The Criminal Justice System Is Racially Biased

- Black and Hispanic suspects are far more likely to be perceived as violent and killed by the police than are White suspects.
- White people are overrepresented as judges, juries, and prosecutors in the criminal justice system, which gives disproportionately long sentences to people of color.
- Stark racial discrepancies appear in drug charges, promoting mass incarceration of people of color while also disqualifying them from the high-profit industry of legalized drugs.

The Debate at a Glance

The Criminal Justice System Is Not Racially Biased

- Research suggests that poverty, not bias, is the driving force of police contact and mass incarceration.
- When suspects are armed or engaging in violent criminal behavior, it is not always clear what is over-policing and what is effective policing.
- Police shootings occur largely with subjects of the same race, minimizing the role of bias in the decision to shoot.

The Criminal Justice System Is Racially Biased

"Our country claims that you are innocent until proven guilty but that is not the case, at least not for a person of color."

—A Black neuroscience student at the University of California, San Francisco

—Anonymous, "Not All Scars Are Visible: A Classmate's Tale of Police Brutality," UCSF Synapse, May 20, 2022. https://synapse.ucsf.edu.

Consider these questions as you read:

1. How might your appearance affect interactions with police?
2. Are there ever situations in which two people who committed the same crime should receive different sentences? Explain your answer.
3. Why do you think people of color make up a greater proportion of those incarcerated for drug charges?

Editor's note: The discussion that follows presents common arguments made in support of this perspective, reinforced by facts, quotes, and examples taken from various sources.

No social justice issues have received more attention in recent years than those of police brutality and a criminal justice system infused with racial bias. Non-White citizens make up about 30 percent of the US population but almost 60 percent of the nation's incarcerated population, according to the National Association for the Advancement of Colored People (NAACP). In fact, further NAACP analysis shows that one out of every seventeen White boys born today can expect to be sentenced to prison at some point in his life; for Latino boys, this number climbs to one in six, and for Black boys, a staggering one in three.

Similar patterns affect other people of color, who are overrepresented in arrests, incarceration, police shootings, and various forms of brutality in the criminal justice system. Dismantling these realities is crucial to the realization of racial justice in America.

Police Contact and Brutality

Black Lives Matter and other social justice movements in recent years have shone a bright light on the incidence of police brutality against Black and Brown Americans. The Mapping Police Violence database reports that as of 2021, Black people comprised 28 percent of those killed by police, despite only being 13 percent of the total US population. In fact, 2021 statistics from the same source show that Black Americans are twice as likely as White Americans to be fatally shot by police.

Latinos also fare poorly in interactions with police. According to the *Washington Post*, in California in 2021 Latinos were 44 percent more likely to be perceived as armed, compared to other ethnic groups. Many cite this bias as part of the reason that, on a national scale, Latinos are killed by police at double the rate that White Americans are. In certain cities, such as Chicago and Minneapolis, Latinos are killed by police at six times the rate of White people.

People of color are aware that racial bias makes them more prone to reactivity from police officers. One Kentucky resident shared in 2020, "As a black man, I'm automatically seen as more suspicious or criminal. [Officers] are already on edge when they approach my car. They're already on edge when they talk to me, when they speak to me. I need to do my best . . . to keep myself at ease, calm, make sure that I don't do anything to set them off."[25]

"As a black man, I'm automatically seen as more suspicious or criminal."[25]

—A Kentucky resident

In fact, by 2018 the American Public Health Association had declared police violence a public health issue—one that particularly afflicts racially marginalized communities. On this large a scale, it is difficult to turn a blind eye to the racial injustice permeating the American criminal justice system.

Biased Juries

Policing is not the only stage of the criminal justice system where bias plays a role: courtrooms also show racially discriminatory

Police Use Disproportionate Force Against People of Color

In 2020 the Prison Policy Initiative analyzed contacts between the police and the public. As a whole, police contacts with each race roughly matched that race's population share. For example, Black people make up about 12 percent of the US population and also make up almost 12 percent of police contacts. However, when the analysts focused on contacts that involved police use of force, an unsettling pattern emerged. Black and Hispanic people were overrepresented in forceful contacts while White people were more likely to have peaceful interactions. Many people cite racial bias for this discrepancy, arguing that racial tensions and assumed criminality make it easier for police contacts with people of color to escalate to violent levels.

Among Individuals Who Have Any Contact with Police, People of Color Disproportionately Experience the Use of Force

	Black	Hispanic	Other	White
People who had any police contact	11.5%	12.5%	6%	70%
People who experienced police use of force	20%	21%	10%	49%

Source: Sawyer, Wendy. "Visualizing the Racial Disparities in Mass Incarceration." Prison Policy Initiative, 27 July 2020, https://www.prisonpolicy.org.

treatment. Evidence shows that non-White people are more likely to be convicted by a jury and receive longer sentences than White people. The US Sentencing Commission confirms that Black offenders receive sentences that are 10 percent longer, on average, than White offenders who committed the same crime.

Minority youth fare even worse in courtroom outcomes. Data from 2021 by the Sentencing Project finds that Latino youth are over 40 percent more likely to be incarcerated than their White peers, with American Indian youth 300 percent more likely, and for Black youth, a whopping 500 percent more likely.

Many attribute these discrepancies to a lack of racial representation in juries. Criminal defendants are guaranteed a jury of their peers (meaning a group of randomized, third-party equals) who will decide whether the defendants are guilty of the charges against them. But courts can exert massive influence on which jurors they deem up to the task of delivering an unbiased opinion. Asking potential jurors whether they have ever had a negative interaction with law enforcement, for example, makes it far more likely that potential jurors of color will be dismissed than prospective White jurors. In fact, one twenty-five-year-long study in Mississippi concluding in 2017 found that Black prospective jurors were removed from juries at four times the rate that Whites were. Thus, rather than providing a jury of true peers, courts may actually exacerbate biases by creating a racial divide between minority defendants and the jury that is tasked with determining their guilt. Indeed, according to the Equal Justice Initiative, "the more White people there are on a jury, the more harshly a Black defendant will be sentenced—especially if the victim is white. Latino defendants also receive longer sentences from majority-white juries."[26]

Racism and Drugs

Many point to the irony of drug charges amid the legalization of marijuana as evidence that the criminal justice system is biased against people of color. While use and consumption of the drug remains illegal on a federal level, thirty-seven states had individually legalized the use of recreational or medical marijuana as of 2022. These states can set standards for how much marijuana an adult can possess at one time and require businesses to obtain a license to sell cannabis products. As such, drug charges are still possible for marijuana users who fail to follow these guidelines.

Arrest rates for marijuana follow a striking racial pattern. A 2020 report by the American Civil Liberties Union found that despite similar marijuana usage among Black and White Americans, Black people were almost four times more likely to be arrested for cannabis possession. In some counties the disparities were so high that Black people were even twenty to fifty times more likely to be arrested. These disparities serve as a "big red flag that policing for cannabis is racially biased,"[27] says *Forbes* contributing writer Emily Earlenbaugh.

Over-policing communities of color for marijuana is particularly devastating because arrest records affect access to legal cannabis industries. In states like California, Colorado, and Nevada, someone with a history of controlled substance offenses is ineligible to obtain a cannabis business license. As a result, White people, who are far more likely to escape drug charges—despite similar rates of drug use—have a near monopoly on the legal cannabis industry. Studies show that up to 90 percent of marijuana dispensaries are owned by White Americans. Kashea McCowan writes for Anti-Racism Daily:

> As a result of the aggressive enforcement of the marijuana possession laws carried out by excessive racial bias, hundreds of thousands of people are thrown into the criminal justice system. . . . The industry that once financially supported and criminalized people of color in low-income communities historically is now being deemed as medicinal when big white corporations, white businesses, and white farmers want to make a profit. Now that marijuana is being legalized, it is becoming harder for people of color to share in the cannabis boom. Government rules will decide who can profit from growing the crop.[28]

In this way discriminatory policing for drugs funnels people of color into incarceration while allowing White users to slide by and even capitalize on the industry. "It is an irony," says *Forbes* writer Joan Oleck, "of gruesome proportions."[29] As states continue to legalize marijuana, it remains to be seen whether these patterns of racially biased arrests will continue.

The Criminal Justice System Is Not Racially Biased

"Advocating for Black lives shouldn't be an invitation to wage a war against police or promote a culture that deliberately and overtly defies authority."

—Jasmine Vaughn-Hall, a Black reporter for *USA Today*

—Jasmine Vaughn-Hall, "From a Cop's Daughter: Saying 'Blue Lives Matter' Doesn't Honor Police. It Divides All of Us," *York Daily Record*, September 21, 2020. www.ydr.com.

Consider these questions as you read:

1. Which do you consider to be the greater influence on interactions with police and the criminal justice system: poverty or race? Explain your answer.
2. Do you agree with the view that high crime rates are more relevant than race in negative interactions with police? Explain your answer.
3. Do you believe overly aggressive policing is a symptom of racial bias? Why or why not?

Editor's note: The discussion that follows presents common arguments made in support of this perspective, reinforced by facts, quotes, and examples taken from various sources.

The reality that people of color are more likely to fare worse in the criminal justice system—from police contact to sentencing decisions—is upsetting. But addressing these discrepancies becomes tricky when legitimate cases of illicit behavior persist. As explained by Brown University economist Glenn C. Loury, police contact depends on "the frequency with which that individual behaves in a manner that attracts police attention. Criminal behavior is not equally distributed across all population groups."[30]

And population groups do not always correlate perfectly to race. Crime follows poverty, trauma, mental illness, and more.

These overlapping factors muddle the conversation of racial discrepancies in criminal justice, an issue America is sorely aching to solve.

Overlap of Poverty and Race

Bias in policing is at the forefront of the conversation of racial justice today. In particular, the Black Lives Matter movement has shed light on the disproportionate number of police shootings of Black Americans. Ample statistics show that police shoot and kill Black suspects at a rate higher than their proportion of the American population. But many scholars find issue with this comparison.

Using metrics like these assumes that every group is exposed to the same amount of police contact, which they are not. Poverty is an overwhelming indicator of whether individuals will interact with police in their lifetime. For this reason, researchers say, we should use *poverty rates*, not *population proportion*, as the benchmark. Otherwise, data on shootings will mix issues of poverty with issues of bias.

Michigan State University psychology professor Joseph Cesario and colleagues put this hypothesis to the test in 2017. The study found that proportional to their population, Black Americans are 2.5 times more likely to be fatally shot by

> "Criminal behavior is not equally distributed across all population groups."[30]
>
> —Glenn C. Loury, Brown University economist

police than White Americans. But Black people are also almost exactly 2.5 times more likely to be poor than White people. Taking these numbers into account, the researchers found that 3.34 out of 100,000 poor Black Americans are killed by police each year, while 3.64 poor White Americans are killed by the police each year. When taking class into account, the anti-Black disparity disappears—even showing a slight anti-White disparity. In fact, poor White citizens are also more likely to be killed by police than middle- or upper-class citizens. This supports poverty, not race, as the driving factor.

Evidence like this does not mean that bias does not exist, but it does highlight a commonly ignored statistical flaw. Growing up in a low-income area increases the likelihood of arrest, and high bail (the average bail bond is $10,000, or eight months of income for the average defendant) ensures that poor people remain behind bars. Furthermore, as explained by the Prison Policy Initiative:

> Poverty is not only a predictor of incarceration; it is also frequently the outcome, as a criminal record and time spent in prison destroys wealth, creates debt, and decimates job opportunities. It's no surprise that people of color—who face much greater rates of poverty—are dramatically overrepresented in the nation's prisons and jails. These racial disparities are particularly stark for Black Americans, who make up 38% of the incarcerated population despite representing only 12% of U.S. residents.[31]

People's Policy Project researcher Nathaniel Lewis found similar explanations for the overrepresentation of Black Americans in prisons. He explains the phenomenon as "primarily a system of managing poor people, rather than black people, and the racial disparities show up mostly because black people are disproportionately represented in the lower classes."[32] The American criminal justice system may not be a racist one, but it is definitely a classist one.

History of Criminal Behavior

For the same reason that Cesario took poverty rates into account in his study of disproportionate police killings, other researchers have done something similar in the context of crime. It is a sad and bitter reality that communities of color tend to experience crime at higher rates than White communities. And when police are called to areas so deeply wrought with street violence, fatal shootings become more likely.

Homicide is the most glaring example. The Giffords Law Center found that Hispanic and Indigenous people in the United States die from homicide at over twice the rate of Whites. Young Black men suffer most severely, dying from homicide at eighteen times the rate of young White men. Heather Mac Donald of the Manhattan Institute explains:

> "The African American community tends to be policed more heavily, because that is where people are disproportionately hurt by violent street crime."[33]
>
> —Heather Mac Donald, Manhattan Institute

Much of modern policing is driven by crime data and community demands for help. The African American community tends to be policed more heavily, because that is where people are disproportionately hurt by violent street crime. In New York City in 2018, 73% of shooting victims were Black, though Black residents comprise only 24% of the city's population. . . . Ideally, officers would never take anyone's life in the course of their duties. But given the number of arrests they make each year (around 10 million) and the number of deadly weapons attacks on officers (an average of 27 per day in just two-thirds of the nation's police departments, according to a 2014 analysis), it is not clear that these . . . civilian shooting deaths [by police] suggest that law enforcement is out of control.[33]

High crime rates make determining bias complicated, particularly when considering that data show that up to 96 percent of police shooting victims were armed. Because disproportionate shootings follow disproportionate danger, the Stanford Open Policing Project says, "disentangling discrimination from effective policing is challenging."[34]

Intraracial Shootings

The image of a White police officer kneeling on the neck of a Black suspect is undeniably haunting. It serves as a chilling

Poverty Is More Significant than Race in Police Shootings

Poverty, not racial bias, may be the biggest driver of police shootings. Using data from a two-year time period, researchers found that while police shot and killed both White people and Black people, every victim had one thing in common: poverty. In fact, no person of any race who lived above the poverty level was killed by police. As such, shootings by law enforcement hardly serve as evidence to a racially biased criminal justice system.

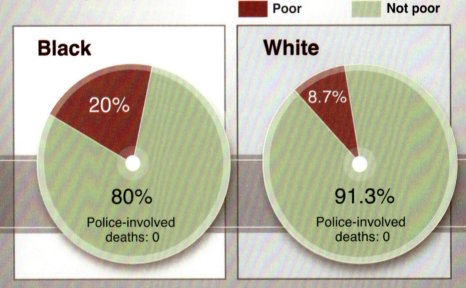

Source: "Poverty Explains Racial Bias in Police Shootings," Index, September 27, 2019. https://replicationindex.com.shootings.

reminder of the power of police. However, that image may also distract from the intraracial violence also widely pervasive in today's system.

In 2019 a group of researchers analyzed over nine hundred fatal US police shootings. They found that officers are more likely to shoot civilians of their own race—meaning that Black officers shoot Black suspects more often, Hispanic officers shoot Hispanic suspects more often, and so forth. This is likely because police precincts tend to reflect the demographic of the areas they serve. Nevertheless, the study was not able to find any anti-Black or anti-Hispanic disparities across police shootings.

Local departments often show this as well. For example, a US Department of Justice study found that White officers in Philadelphia were actually less likely to shoot an unarmed Black suspect than were either Black or Hispanic officers. Stories like these can easily get lost when only looking at collective national data.

Of course, even intraracial shootings may serve as a sign of an overly aggressive policing culture. But if racial tension was the predominant source of these shootings, then it would be strange to see people of color most often shot by someone of their own race. As Mac Donald notes, "However sickening the video of Floyd's arrest, it isn't representative of the 375 million annual contacts that police officers have with civilians. A solid body of evidence finds no structural bias in the criminal-justice system with regards to arrests, prosecution or sentencing."[35]

Source Notes

Overview: Racial Justice

1. Derald Wing Sue, "What Is a Microaggression? What to Know About These Everyday Slights," Health Matters, December 10, 2020. https://healthmatters.nyp.org.
2. Warren Ng, "'Death by a Thousand Cuts': The Impact of Microaggressions on the AAPI Community," Health Matters, May 25, 2021. https://healthmatters.nyp.org.
3. Theodore R. Johnson, "To Realize Justice, We Must Confront Racism," Brennan Center for Justice, April 20, 2021. www.brennancenter.org.

Chapter One: Is Racial Bias Preventing Some Americans from Achieving Economic Progress?

4. Langston Hughes, *Harlem*, Poetry Foundation. www.poetryfoundation.org.
5. Quoted in *Segregated by Design*, directed by Mark Lopez, 2019. www.segregatedbydesign.com.
6. Quoted in Nick Adjami, "'She's Definitely African': One Person's Experience with Housing Discrimination," Equal Rights Center, February 27, 2020. https://equalrightscenter.org.
7. Quoted in Adjami, "'She's Definitely African.'"
8. Emmanuel Martinez and Lauren Kirchner, "The Secret Bias Hidden in Mortgage-Approval Algorithms," The Markup, August 25, 2021. https://themarkup.org.
9. Robin Bleiweis et al., "Women of Color and the Wage Gap," Center for American Progress, November 17, 2021. www.americanprogress.org.
10. Quoted in Gwen Aviles, "Advocates Say Latinas Who Make Less than Their White Colleagues Are 'Screaming into the Void' on Equal Pay Day," Insider, October 22, 2021. www.insider.com.
11. Quoted in Tracy Jan, "13 Million People in Poverty Are Disconnected from the Social Safety Net. Most of Them Are White," *Washington Post*, February 4, 2019. www.washingtonpost.com.
12. Peter H. Schuck, "What Systemic Racism Systematically Downplays," National Affairs, 2022. www.nationalaffairs.com.

Chapter Two: Does Affirmative Action Promote Racial Justice?

13. Public Papers of the Presidents of the United States: Lyndon B. Johnson, 1965. Volume II. Washington, DC: Government Printing Office, 1966, pp. 635–40. www.lbjlib.utexas.edu.
14. Connor Maxwell and Sara Garcia, "5 Reasons to Support Affirmative Action in College Admissions," Center for American Progress, October 1, 2019. www.americanprogress.org.
15. Quoted in Grace Baek, "Affirmative Action and the Diversity Dilemma," CBS News, April 15, 2021. www.cbsnews.com.
16. Sheen S. Levine and David Stark, "Diversity Makes You Brighter," *New York Times*, December 9, 2015. www.nytimes.com.
17. Ryan Keane, "Affirmative Action: Failed Promises & The Brighter Future," *Berkeley Political Review*, October 28, 2020. https://bpr.berkeley.edu.
18. James E. Cherry, "White Privilege: The Original Affirmative Action," *Jackson (TN) Sun*, July 27, 2018. www.jacksonsun.com.
19. Louis Menand, "The Changing Meaning of Affirmative Action," *New Yorker*, January 13, 2020. www.newyorker.com.
20. Keane, "Affirmative Action."
21. Quoted in Baek, "Affirmative Action and the Diversity Dilemma."
22. Chris Talgo, "Base College Admissions on Merit," *Charleston (SC) Post and Courier*, September 14, 2020. www.postandcourier.com.
23. Quoted in Kirk Carapezza, "As Supreme Court Weighs Harvard Admissions Case, Two Asian Americans Speak Out and Allege Bias," GBH, July 22, 2021. www.wgbh.org.
24. Keane, "Affirmative Action."

Chapter Three: Is the Criminal Justice System Racially Biased?

25. Quoted in Kristen Edwards, "'The Talk': Black Families Teach Their Children How to Survive Police Encounters," WLEX, June 9, 2020. www.lex18.com.
26. Equal Justice Initiative, *Race and the Jury: Illegal Racial Discrimination in Jury Selection*, 2021. https://eji.org.
27. Emily Earlenbaugh, "Seth Rogen Says Racist Cannabis Policing Harms Black Community, but Expungement Can Help," *Forbes*, July 16, 2020. www.forbes.com.
28. Kashea McCowan, "The Legalization of Marijuana Still Doesn't Include Everyone," Anti-Racism Daily, April 20, 2022. https://the-ard.com.

29. Joan Oleck, "With 40,000 Americans Incarcerated for Marijuana Offenses, the Cannabis Industry Needs to Step Up, Activists Said This Week," *Forbes*, June 26, 2020. www.forbes.com.
30. Glenn C. Loury and Peter Winkler, "Racism Is an Empty Thesis," *City Journal*, June 11, 2020. www.city-journal.org.
31. Wendy Sawyer and Peter Wagner, "Mass Incarceration: The Whole Pie 2022," Prison Policy Initiative, March 14, 2022. www.prison policy.org.
32. Quoted in Zaid Jilani, "New Report Finds Class Is a More Potent Predictor of Incarceration than Race. But Racism Drives It," The Intercept, February 5, 2018. https://theintercept.com.
33. Heather Mac Donald, "There Is No Epidemic of Fatal Police Shootings Against Unarmed Black Americans," Manhattan Institute, July 3, 2020. www.manhattan-institute.org.
34. Stanford Open Policing Project, "Findings," 2021. https://open policing.stanford.edu.
35. Heather Mac Donald, "The Myth of Systemic Police Racism," *Wall Street Journal*, June 2, 2020. www.wsj.com.

Racial Justice Facts

Sentencing

- The Council on Criminal Justice found in 2019 that prison time among Black people had increased by 1 percent or more each year from 2000 to 2016.
- Kristin Henning shares in her 2021 book *The Rage of Innocence* that Black children make up 51 percent of the cases that judges choose to transfer from a juvenile court to be tried as an adult.
- The Southern Coalition for Social Justice finds that 80 percent of defendants who receive the death penalty are people of color.
- Because of laws that disenfranchise people with felony convictions, one in thirteen Black people of voting age are denied the right to vote, as found by the Drug Policy Alliance in 2018.

Workplace

- According to McKinsey & Company, Black people make up less than 7 percent of the managerial workforce and only about 1 percent of Fortune 500 chief executive officer spots.
- McKinsey & Company estimates that it will take another ninety-five years for Black employees to become proportional to workers of other races in the private sector.
- The National Women's Law Center estimates that over the course of a forty-year career, Black women lose almost $1 million in wage discrepancies.
- One study by law professor Joan C. Williams found that the performance evaluations of employees of color mentioned mistakes 43 percent of the time, but only 26 percent of the time in evaluations of White men.

Violence

- The Federal Bureau of Investigation found that in 2019, hate crimes reached their highest levels since 2008; bias-based murders even doubled from 2018.
- In 2016 the US Department of Justice found that Native American women were up to three times more likely to be assaulted than women of other races.
- Ninety-six percent of Native American women who have been assaulted identify their attacker as non-Native American.
- In 2017 more than two thousand Jewish community centers received bomb threats.

Wealth

- The Century Foundation found in 2016 that one in thirteen White Americans live in high-poverty neighborhoods. For Hispanic Americans, this number climbs to one in six, and for Black Americans, one in four.
- Black-owned banks control $4.8 billion, which is less than 1 percent of America's banking assets, according to a 2020 NPR report.
- The 2018 census found Native Americans to have the highest poverty rate of any minority group.
- In 2022 Latinos were the ethnic group with the fastest-growing homeownership rate. The Urban Institute projects that by 2040, 70 percent of new homeowner households will be Latino.

Public Attitudes

- The NAACP finds that 65 percent of Black adults have felt targeted because of their race. The same is true for approximately 35 percent of Latino and Asian adults.
- A 2020 Gallup poll found that just 19 percent of Black adults had confidence in law enforcement.
- In 2021 almost 80 percent of Americans believed that racial discrimination was a problem in the United States, according to a Monmouth University poll.

Related Organizations and Websites

American Civil Liberties Union

www.aclu.org

The American Civil Liberties Union was founded in 1920 to support the civil rights of all Americans. The union provides news, videos, court cases, press releases, and more pertaining to racial justice.

Black Lives Matter (BLM)

https://blacklivesmatter.com

Black Lives Matter was founded in 2013 in response to the acquittal of the man who shot and killed Trayvon Martin. Since then, BLM has become a global human rights movement whose mission is the eradication of White supremacy. Signing up on the BLM website provides updates on special launches, network actions, programs, partnerships, and more.

Color of Change

www.colorofchange.org

Color of Change is an online organization driven by over 7 million members to help Black people and others respond to all forms of injustice. The website allows anyone to start a petition for a campaign of choice, reaching its audience of millions as well as providing help from experts if needed.

Equal Justice Initiative (EJI)

https://eji.org

The EJI is a nonprofit organization founded in 1989 that provides legal representation to people who have been wrongly convicted or otherwise abused by the American criminal justice system. The organization is committed to changing the country's narrative on race and crime.

Kirwan Institute for the Study of Race and Ethnicity

https://kirwaninstitute.osu.edu

The Kirwan Institute for the Study of Race and Ethnicity is a research institute at Ohio State University. It provides information on research initiatives, training and resources, programs, and more that help build the capacity of allied racial justice campaigns.

Know Your Rights Camp

www.knowyourrightscamp.com

Know Your Rights Camp is a free campaign founded by Colin Kaepernick that helps educate youth on how to have safe interactions with law enforcement and also empowers them to demand equal treatment regardless of their race.

National Association for the Advancement of Colored People (NAACP)

https://naacp.org

The NAACP is a long-standing civil rights organization with a mission to address racism in criminal justice, education, health care, climate, and other key areas. Its website includes information on voting rights, federal courts, voting records in Congress, and more.

Poverty and Race Research Action Council

www.prrac.org

The Poverty and Race Research Action Council provides a collection of readings on topics related to racial justice, including fair housing, school diversity, environmental justice, and civil rights history.

Race Forward

www.raceforward.org

Race Forward is an organization committed to the systemic analysis of complex race issues. In 2017 it united with the Center for Social Inclusion, which shares the goal of creating equitable outcomes for all. Together, these organizations present Facing Race, which is the largest multiracial conference on racial justice in the United States.

For Further Research

Books

Leanne Currie-McGhee, *Stand Up for Racial Justice*. San Diego: ReferencePoint, 2022.

Barbara Diggs, *Racial Bias: Is Change Possible?* San Diego: ReferencePoint, 2023.

Harvard Business Review et al., *Racial Justice: The Insights You Need from* Harvard Business Review. Boston: Harvard Business School, 2021.

Kristin Henning, *Rage of Innocence: How America Criminalizes Black Youth*. New York: Vintage, 2022.

Olivia Karson, *Thinking Critically: The Black Lives Matter Movement*. San Diego: ReferencePoint, 2023.

Philip Leigh, *The Dreadful Frauds: Critical Race Theory and Identity Politics*. Columbia, SC: Shotwell, 2022.

Bettina Love, *We Want to Do More than Survive: Abolitionist Teaching and the Pursuit of Educational Freedom*. Boston: Beacon, 2020.

Heather Mac Donald, *The Diversity Delusion: How Race and Gender Pandering Corrupt the University and Undermine Our Culture*. New York: St. Martin's, 2020.

Internet Sources

N. Jamiyla Chisholm, "Reform, Abolish or Defund the Police—Explained," Colorlines, August 3, 2020. www.colorlines.com.

Malkia Derich Cyril et al., "Mismatched—Philanthropy's Response to the Call for Racial Justice," Philanthropic Initiative for Racial Equity, 2021. https://racialequity.org.

Xavier De Souza Briggs and Lora-Ellen McKinney, "Impunity Is a Kill Switch for Racial Progress," *Boston Globe*, April 24, 2022. www.bostonglobe.com.

Government Alliance on Race & Equity, "Juneteenth: A First Step in the Long Work of Atonement," June 19, 2022. www.racial equityalliance.org.

Philanthropic Initiative for Racial Equity, "Racial Justice Organizations and Resources." https://racialequity.org.

Shani Saxon, "Economist Finds Cost of Racial Bias to Be $16 Trillion in Losses," Colorlines, October 23, 2020. www.colorlines .com.

Robert VerBruggen et al., "Which Black Lives Matter?," Manhattan Institute, May 3, 2022. www.manhattan-institute.org.

Frederick F. Wherry, "Where Credit Scores Come from and Why They Don't Quite Add Up—but Can," *Boston Globe*, May 30, 2022. www.bostonglobe.com.

Index

Picture Credits

Cover: FilippoBacci/iStock

8: Sheila Fitzgerald/Shutterstock.com

17: Maury Aaseng

21: Maury Aaseng

29: Maury Aaseng

36: Maury Aaseng

41: Maury Aaseng

48: Maury Aaseng

About the Author

Olivia Karson is a University of California, Davis graduate with degrees in economics and political science. Her emphases include American history and human rights studies. Karson is also the author of *Thinking Critically: The Black Lives Matter Movement*. She lives in San Diego, California.